# THE MUSIC QUOTATION BOOK

# The Music Quotation Book

*A Literary Fanfare*

Edited by

JOYCE AND MAURICE LINDSAY

ROBERT HALE · LONDON

*Preface and selection © Joyce and Maurice Lindsay 1992*
*First published in Great Britain 1992*
*Reprinted 1993 (four times)*
*Reprinted 1994 (twice)*

10  12  14  15  13  11  9

Robert Hale Limited
Clerkenwell House
Clerkenwell Green
London EC1R 0HT

The right of Joyce and Maurice Lindsay to be identified
as authors of this work has been asserted by them
in accordance with the Copyright, Designs
and Patents Act 1988.

Printed and bound
in Great Britain by
WBC Bookbinders Ltd.

# Preface

here words leave off, music begins,' declared the poet Heinrich Heine. That being so, it seemed pointless to print words, however poetically beautiful, in praise of music. Instead, we have concentrated on the varieties of wit that music and musicians have inspired. Some of it is savage, reflecting the animosities composers lavished on their contemporaries, or with which critics have alike belaboured composers and performers. In the light of so much amusing invective, 'A Handful of Wrong Notes' might seem a suitable subtitle for this book. Some of the wit, however, is more genial, designed to amuse rather than coruscate.

The provenance of many of these stories, circulating among musicians and their audiences, is often hard to trace. The pointed wisdom of Corno di Basseto, alias George Bernard Shaw has, of course, been collected, as have the elegant shafts of humour so regularly despatched by Sir Thomas Beecham (though many, possibly apocryphal, Beecham stories survive in aural tradition).

We are grateful to copyright holders who freely gave permission for the use of the material in this book: to The Society of Authors for the use of the quotations by Bernard Shaw; to Julia MacRae Books for the Gerald Moore quotations; to Bernard Levin and the *Sunday Times* and *The Times*.

Every effort was made to communicate with all copyright holders. We offer our apologies to those we may have overlooked or whom we were unable to trace.

JOYCE and MAURICE LINDSAY

# Concert

Stroking at strings to make a singing edge
or channelling their fingered breath through gauge
of ebony or brass, musicians play,
as if what they produced was workaday.
Tribally, the audience, unaware
it looks absurd, sits in a motionless stare –
till out of disappointments, hungers, aches
of body, self-tormenting fret, there wakes
the gift of love, a tremble of elation,
a sudden, strange fulfilling agitation,
some brief content not ours to have or hold
touching on meanings words must leave untold.
MAURICE LINDSAY
*Collected Poems 1940–90*

Music is a strange thing.
> LORD BYRON
> *Diary*, 21 February 1821

Music's a rum go!
> attributed to RALPH VAUGHAN WILLIAMS

If I were to begin life again, I would devote it to music. It is the only cheap and unpunished rapture on earth.
> SYDNEY SMITH
> in a letter to the Countess of Carlisle, 1844

Music alone has the power to make us penetrate into ourselves; the other arts offer us only eccentric pleasures.
> HONORÉ DE BALZAC
> *Cambara*

(Music) is the only sensual pleasure without vice.
> SAMUEL JOHNSON
> Mary Hawkins: *Johnsoniana*, 1787

Music helps not the toothache.
> GEORGE HERBERT
> *Jacula Prudentum*, 1651

Music is the refuge of souls ulcerated by happiness.
> E.M. CORIAN
> *Syllogismes de l'amertume*

Tonight he said that 'if he had learnt music, he should have been afraid he should have done nothing else but play. It was a method of employing the mind, without the labour of thinking at all, and with some applause from a man's self.'
SAMUEL JOHNSON
quoted in Boswell's *Journal of a Tour to the Hebrides*

Music is a beautiful opiate, if you don't take it too seriously.
HENRY MILLER
*The Air-conditioned Nightmare*

To me music is a noise more important than agreeable.
MARIE ANNE DU DEFFAND
*Correspondence inédite*, 1859

Music is the only noise for which one is obliged to pay.
attributed to ALEXANDRE DUMAS

Music is a pastime, a relaxation from more serious pursuits.
ALEXANDER BOUDON
*Letter to V. A. Krylov*, 1867

Music is the most disagreeable and the most widely beloved of all noises.
THÉOPHILE GAUTIER
*Le Figaro*, 20 October 1863

Much music marreth men's manners.
GALEN
quoted in Roger Ascham's *Toxophilius*, 1545

Music is the eye of the ear.
THOMAS DRAXE
*Bibliotheca*, 1616

A taste of sculpture and painting is in my mind as becoming as a taste of fiddling and piping is unbecoming a man of fashion. The former is connected with history and poetry, the latter with nothing that I know of but bad company.

> LORD CHESTERFIELD
> *Letter to his Son*, 1744

Too many pieces [of music] finish too long after the end.

> IGOR STRAVINSKY
> quoted in the *New York Review of Books*

Musick is the exaltation of poetry. Both of them may excel apart, but surely they are most excellent when they are joyn'd, because nothing is then wanting to either of their proportions; for thus they appear like wit and beauty in the same person.

> HENRY PURCELL
> Preface to *Dioclesian*, 1690

Learn thoroughly how to compose a fugue, and then *don't*.
> BERNARD SHAW
> *How to Become a Music Critic*

So your fugue broadens and thickens,
Greatens and deepens and lengthens,
Till one exclaims – 'But where's music, the dickens?'
> ROBERT BROWNING
> *Master Hughes of Saxe-Gotha*

A fugue is a piece of music in which the voices come in one after another and the audience go out one after another.
> ANON

Composers shouldn't think too much – it interferes with their plagiarism.
> HOWARD DIETZ

All music with a centre is tonal. Music without a centre is fine for a moment or two, but it soon sounds all the same.
> ALAN HOVHANESS

There is one objection to atonalism so simple and childish that no one seems to have had the courage to make it ... it has produced nothing that we can set beside Chabrier and Offenbach, let alone the comic operas of Mozart ... Atonalism, though plastic in minor details of texture, is in fact the least flexible and most monotonous of media, and for that reason alone it is unlikely to play much part in the music of the future.
> CONSTANT LAMBERT
> *Music Ho!*

Can't you listen to chords without knowing their names?
    CLAUDE DEBUSSY
    quoted in *La Revue Musicale*


Ragtime came squirting out of the pianola in gushes of treacle and hot perfume.
    ALDOUS HUXLEY
    *Crome Yellow*


It was delightful, too, for people without a vestige of talent ... who could just strum a tune or string a few lines of doggerel, to be told that all that distinguishes what used to be called 'serious art' from their productions was of no consequence whatever and that, on the contrary, it was these ... that ought to be taken seriously ... The encouragement given to fatuous ignorance to swell with admiration at its own incompetence is perhaps what has turned most violently so many intelligent and sensitive people against Jazz. They see that it encourages thousands of the stupid and vulgar to fancy that they can understand art, and hundreds of the conceited to imagine that they can create it.
    CLIVE BELL
    *Since Cézanne: 'Plus de Jazz'*


Jazz – music invented by demons for the torture of imbeciles.
    HENRY VAN DYKE


Jazz will endure just as long as people hear it through their feet instead of their brains.
    JOHN PHILIP SOUSA

One can reject jazz, but only the blind and the deaf will ignore it.
> KURT HONOLKA
> *Musik in unser Zeit*

Popular music is popular because a lot of people like it.
> IRVING BERLIN

Pop music is very disposable, that's the great thing about it.
> ELTON JOHN

I don't know anything about music. In my line you don't have to.
> ELVIS PRESLEY

Musicke might tame and civilize wild beasts, but 'tis evident it never could tame and civilize musicians.
> JOHN GAY

The Italians exalt music; the French enliven it; the Germans strive after it; and the English pay for it well.
> GEORG MATHESON
> *Neueröffnete Orchester*, 1713

> A squeak is heard in the orchestra
> As the leader draws across
> The intestines of the agile cat
> The tail of the noble hoss.
>> GEORGE T. LANIGAN
>> from *Sweet and Sour*

Modern music covers a multitude of dins.
> a misprint in a Scottish local paper

Three farts and a raspberry, orchestrated.
SIR JOHN BARBIROLLI on modern music
quoted in Michael Kennedy's *Barbirolli: Conductor Laureate*

I don't think that there was ever a piece of music that changed a man's decision on how to vote.
ARTUR SCHNABEL
*My Life in Music*

For I consider music as a very innocent diversion and perfectly compatible with the profession of a clergyman.
JANE AUSTEN
*Pride and Prejudice*

It is very odd about George and music. You know his parents were quite normal – liked horses and dogs, and the country.
DUKE OF WINDSOR of George Lascelles, 7th Earl of Harewood
quoted by Shirley Lowe, *The Times*, 'Hedgehogs and High Notes', 23 June 1983

Some men are like musical glasses – to produce their finest tones you must keep them wet.
SAMUEL TAYLOR COLERIDGE

Some music is above me; most music is beneath me.
SAMUEL TAYLOR COLERIDGE
*Table Talk*, 6 July 1833

The Opera ... proceeds upon a false estimate of taste and morals; it supposes that the capacity for enjoyment may be multiplied with the objects calculated to afford it. It is a species of intellectual prostitution; for we can no more

16

receive pleasure from all our faculties at once than we can
be in love with a number of mistresses at the same time.
>    WILLIAM HAZLITT
>    'The Opera', *Essays*

There's two kinds of music, good and bad. If you like it, it's
good – if you don't, it's bad.
>    HARRY JAMES
>    quoted by Robin Ray in *Words on Music*

My favourite music is the sound of radio commercials at ten
dollars a whack.
>    LORD THOMSON OF FLEET

The general aim in music is to make other people feel
outsiders.
>    STEPHEN POTTER
>    *Lifemanship*

Music is ... well, I *know* it's better than working in Fords.
IAN DURY

Is it not strange that sheeps' guts should hale souls out of
men's bodies?
WILLIAM SHAKESPEARE
*Much Ado About Nothing*

All Paradise opens! Let me die eating ortolans to the sound
of soft music!
BENJAMIN DISRAELI
*The Young Duke*, 1830

*All*: The music ho!
*Cleopatra*: Let it alone; let's to billiards.
WILLIAM SHAKESPEARE
*Antony and Cleopatra*

God save me from a bad neighbour and a beginner on the
fiddle.
ITALIAN PROVERB

In came a fiddler – and tuned like fifty stomache-aches.
CHARLES DICKENS
*A Christmas Carol*

There is nothing, I think, in which the power of art is
shown so much as in playing the fiddle. In all other things
we can do something at first. Any man will forge a bar of
iron, if you give him a box, though a clumsy one; but give
him a fiddle, and a fiddle-stick and he can do nothing.
JAMES BOSWELL
*Life of Johnson, 1791*

An ordinary fiddler makes better music for a shilling than a gentleman will do after spending forty.
SAMUEL PEPYS
*Diary*

I do play the violin, but not well enough to hold a steady job – just a series of one night stands.
world famous violinist ISAAC STERN

Madam, you have between your legs an instrument capable of giving pleasure to thousands – and all you can do is scratch it.
attributed to SIR THOMAS BEECHAM
to a lady cellist during a rehearsal

Imagine with yourself what an unsightly matter it were to see a woman play upon a tabour or drums, or like instrument; and this because the boisterousness of them doth both cover and take away that sweet mildness which setteth so forth every deed that a woman doth.

> BALDASSARE CASTIGLIONE
> *Libro del Cortegiano*, translated by Sir Thomas Hogy, 1561

The world is a difficult world, indeed,
And people are hard to suit,
And the man who plays on the violin
Is a bore to the man with the flute.

> SIR THOMAS BEECHAM
> Atkins and Newman, *Beecham Stories*

A tutor who tooted the flute,
Tried to teach two young tooters to toot;
Said the two to the tutor,
'Is it harder to toot or
To tutor two tooters to toot?'

> CAROLYN WELLS
> quoted Logue, *Sweet and Sour*, 1983

The Hautboys who played to us last night had their breath froze in their instruments, till it dropt off the ends of 'em in icicles by god this is true.

> WILLIAM CONGREVE
> *Letter to Edward Porter*, 15 January 1700

An oboe is an ill-wind that nobody blows good.

> BENNETT CERF
> *Laughing Stock*, 1952

'They should have stuck to strings as we did, and kept out clarinets, and done away with serpents. If you'd thrive in musical religion, stick to strings, say I.'

'Strings be safe soul-lifters, as far as that do go,' said Mrs Spinks.

'Yet there's worse things than serpents,' said Mrs Penny. 'Old things pass away, 'tis true; but a serpent was a good old note: a deep rich note was a serpent.'

'Clar'nets, however, be bad at all times,' said Michael Mail.

'One Christmas – years agone now, years – I went the rounds wi' the Weatherbury quire. 'Twas a hard frosty night, and the keys of all the clarinets froze, so that 'twas like drawing a cork every time a key was opened.'

THOMAS HARDY
*Under the Greenwood Tree*

The Wedding-Guest here beat his breast,
For he heard the loud bassoon.
    SAMUEL TAYLOR COLERIDGE
    *The Ancient Mariner*


At the close of the first movement the principal horn called
out to one of the first violins, 'Tom, have you been able to
discover a tune yet?' 'I have not,' was Tom's reply.
    Account of an early rehearsal of Schubert's
    Symphony No. 9 in C, *Musical Times*, February 1897


Never let the horns and woodwinds out of your sight. If you
can hear them at all, they are too loud.
    RICHARD STRAUSS
    *Ten Golden Rules Inscribed in the Album of a Young*
    *Conductor*, 1927


The tuba is certainly the most intestinal of instruments, the
very lowest bowel of music.
    PETER DE VRIES
    *The Glory of the Hummingbird*, 1974


'Are you producing as much sound as possible from that
quaint and antique drainage system which you are applying
to your face?'
    SIR THOMAS BEECHAM, to a trombone-player
    Atkins and Newman, *Beecham Stories*


What can yield a tone so like an eunuch's voice as a true
cornet pipe?
    ROGER NORTH
    *The Musical Grammarian*, 1728

He promptly made a trumpet of his arse.
>    DANTE
>    *The Inferno*, Canto XXI

My bowels shall sound like a harp.
>    THE BIBLE, *Isaiah*

What is a harp but an over-sized cheese-slicer with cultural pretensions?
>    DENIS NORDEN
>    *You Can't Have Your Kayak and Heat It*

Joking apart, Prince Albert asked me to go to him on Saturday at two o'clock so that I may try his organ.
>    FELIX MENDELSSOHN

'An organist an accomplished man!' Lady Gosstre repeated Adela's words. 'Well, I suppose it is possible, but it rather upsets one's notions, does it not?'

> GEORGE MEREDITH
> *Sandra Belloni*, 1889

He is verye often drunke and by means thereof he hathe by unorderlye playing on the organ, putt the quire out of time and disordered them.

> Report by Thomas Kingston, organist of Lincoln Cathedral 1599–1616, in *The Chapter of Lincoln Minute Book*

Playing a bird-cage with a toasting fork.
Two skeletons copulating on a galvanised tin roof.

> SIR THOMAS BEECHAM of the harpsichord

Musician and logician both
John Wynal lieth here
Who made the organs erst to speak
As if, or as it were.
  Epitaph on John Wynal, organist at York Minster, *c.*
  1573

We had the music of the bagpipe every day at Armidale, Dunvegan and Coll. Dr Johnson appeared fond of it and used often to stand for some time with his ear close to the great drone.
  JAMES BOSWELL
  *Journal of a Tour to the Hebrides*

The bagpipes sound exactly the same when you have finished learning them as when you start.
  SIR THOMAS BEECHAM
  Atkins and Newman, *Beecham Stories*

I find brass bands have a melancholy sound. All right out of doors, of course – fifty miles away. Like bagpipes, they turn what had been a dream into a public nuisance.
  SIR THOMAS BEECHAM
  Atkins and Newman, *Beecham Stories*

I got to try the bagpipes. It was like trying to blow an octopus.
  JAMES GALWAY
  *An Autobiography*, 1978

As the bagpiper was playing, an elderly Gentleman informed us, that in some remote time, the Macdonalds of Glengary having been injured, or offended by the inhabitants of Culloden, and resolving to have justice or vengeance, came to Culloden on a Sunday, where finding their enemies at worship, they shut them up in the church, which they set on fire; and this, said he, is the tune that the piper played while they were burning.

> SAMUEL JOHNSON
> *Journey to the Western Isles*

The vile belchings of the lunatic accordions.

> ARTHUR HONEGGER
> *I Am A Composer*, 1911

A musical growth found adhering to the walls of most semi-detached houses in the provinces.

> SIR THOMAS BEECHAM on upright pianos

I wish the Government would put a tax on pianos for the incompetent

> EDITH SITWELL
> *Selected Letters 1916–1964*

I have a reasonable good ear in music: let us have the tongs and the bones.

> WILLIAM SHAKESPEARE
> *A Midsummer Night's Dream*

A fabulously wealthy lady demanded Kreisler's services, and would not be deterred even when he quoted a fee of $3000 for playing just a few little pieces. The lady then told him that she did not wish him to mix with the guests, many of whom would be very prominent people. He replied immediately: 'In that case, madam, my fee will be only $2000.'

> DONALD BROOK
> *Violinists of To-day*

A friend of mine was serving in the 1914–18 War. Hearing that he was a famous violinist, a Tommy one night in a canteen pressed a fiddle into his hands with only one string to it – the G string – and said, 'Give us the 1812 Overture, mate.'

> GERALD MOORE
> *The Unashamed Accompanist*

Gabor Egervari, the violinist delivering Bartok and Kodaly with fine feeling in the cafés around Budapest's Opera House by night, is a plumber by day and a taxi-driver at the weekend. 'I come as a package,' he remarked. 'I play at weddings, drive the bride and groom home and promise to mend their pipes, all as part of the same deal.'

> ANNE McELVEY
> *The Times*, 29 January 1992

When I am asked if a young player should become a professional pianist, I say if there is any way out, then for heaven's sake no.

> TAMAS VASARY in 1976
> quoted Dean Elder, *Pianists at Bay*

In Geneva, I couldn't practise in the hall the day of my concert because a ballet was performing. At my concert, in the evening, the piano sounded choked. As I continued to play, I saw something sticking out of the sounding board; so after the first movement, I quickly pulled the thing out – it was the corset of a ballet dancer.

> RUDOLPH SERKIN in 1970
> quoted Elder, *Pianists at Bay*

Please do not shoot the pianist. He is doing his best.

> OSCAR WILDE

The great writer on music, Professor Donald Francis Tovey, finished playing a Mozart Piano Concerto in St Andrew's Hall, Glasgow, having conducted the Scottish Orchestra from the keyboard. There were identical doors at both sides of the platform, one the exit to the Green Room, the other leading only into a balancing cul-de-sac. To the concern of the orchestra and the audience, Tovey finished acknowledging the applause and disappeared through the exit leading nowhere, hotly pursued by the leader, Henri Temianka. 'Sir Donald,' said Temianka, 'you can't get out this way.' 'I know that,' said Tovey. 'I just wanted to spit.'

    told by Henri Temianka to Maurice Lindsay in 1936

A German singer! I should as soon expect pleasure from the neighing of my horse.

    FREDERICK THE GREAT of Prussia

I cannot forbear thinking that the Cat-call is originally a Piece of English Musick. Its resemblance to the voice of some of our British songsters as well as the use of it, which is peculiar to our nation, confirms me in this opinion.

    JOSEPH ADDISON
    *The Spectator*, 24 April 1712

I see you have a singing face – a heavy, dull, sonata face.

    GEORGE FARQUHAR
    *The Inconstant*, 1702

She was a town and country soprano of the kind often used for augmenting grief at a funeral.

    GEORGE ADE, *c*. 1928

Her voice produced a precisely similar effect upon the ear which a dull razor might produce on the skin.

    an anonymous music critic in a local paper, *c*. 1930

People applaud a primadonna as they do the feats of a
strong man at the fair. The sensations are painfully
disagreeable, hard to condone, but one is so glad when it is
all over that one cannot help rejoicing.
  JEAN-JACQUES ROUSSEAU
  *La Nouvelle Héloise*, 1761

A young friend of mine was playing the accompaniment …
of Wolf's song 'Bitt ihn, O Mutter' (Beg him, O Mother).
The accompaniment is written with Wolf's usual eloquence
and urgency, but it was played by this young lady with such

viciousness that I ventured to ask her what 'Bitt ihn, O Mutter' meant. 'Of course,' she replied, 'it means, "O mother, bite him".'

GERALD MOORE
*The Unashamed Accompanist*

A vile beastly rottenheaded foolbegotten brazenthroated pernicious piggish screaming, tearing, roaring, perplexing splitmecrackle, crashmewriggle insane ass of a woman is practising howling below-stairs with a brute of a singing master so horrible that my head is nearly off.

EDWARD LEAR
*Letter to Lady Strachey*, 1859

Hell is full of musical amateurs: music is the brandy of the damned.

BERNARD SHAW
*Man and Superman*, 1903

The higher the voice the smaller the intellect.
>attributed to Sir Ernest Newman

As you walk on to the stage, *do not* step on the soprano's train.
>GERALD MOORE
>*The Unashamed Accompanist*

Learning music by reading about it is like making love by mail.
>ISAAC STERN
>quoted Ayre, *The Wit of Music*

I have found nothing more difficult in practising music, than skipping from one part to the other, and keeping my eye on the whole score at once.
>JEAN-JACQUES ROUSSEAU
>*Confessions*

Cherubini was one day confronted by one who believed himself to possess a very good voice, but was uncertain whether he was a tenor or a baritone. This French singer ... opened his mouth, and the foundations ... trembled with the bellowing.
>'What shall I become?' he asked when he had finished.
>'An auctioneer,' replied Cherubini.
>>F.J. CROWEST
>>*Maria Luigi Carlo Zenobi Salvatore Cherubini*, 1926

The King bathes and with great success; a machine follows the Royal one into the sea, filled with fiddlers, who play 'God Save the King' as His Majesty takes the plunge.
>FANNY BURNEY
>*Diary*, 8 July 1789

If nobody wants to go to your concert, nothing will stop them.

ISAAC STERN

I occasionally play works by contemporary composers and for two reasons. First, to discourage the composer from writing any more, and secondly, to remind myself how much I appreciate Beethoven.

JASCHA HEIFETZ
*Life*, 1961

'Getting into the key of C sharp,' he said, 'is like an unprotected female travelling on the Metropolitan Railway, and finding herself at Shepherd's Bush, without quite knowing where she wants to go. How is she ever to get safe back to Clapham Junction? And Clapham Junction won't quite do either, for Clapham Junction is like the diminished seventh – susceptible of such enharmonic change that you can resolve it into all the possible termini of music.'

SAMUEL BUTLER
*The Way of All Flesh*

Nowadays what is not worth saying is sung.

BEAUMARCHAIS
*Le Mariage de Figaro*

Let a man try the very uttermost to speak what he means, before singing is had recourse to.

THOMAS CARLYLE
*Journal*, 1843

Swans sing before they die – 'twere no bad thing
Should certain persons die before they sing.

S.T. COLERIDGE

Tenors get women by the score.
JAMES JOYCE
*Ulysses*

A tenor is not a man but a disease.
attributed to HANS VON BÜLOW

You know my pretensions to musical taste are merely a few of Nature's instincts untaught and untutored by Art. For this reason, many musical compositions, particularly when much of the merit lies in Counterpoint, affect my simple lug no otherwise than as melodious din.
ROBERT BURNS
in a letter to George Thomson, September 1792

His song began with the assertion that he was a soldier … as he was a weedy individual … wearing steel-framed spectacles, the audience refused to accept his statement.
SIR HARRY LAUDER
*Roamin' in the Gloamin'*

I would rather hear 'Annie Lauder' sung with feeling than the greatest singer in the world declaiming a scene from *Tristan and Isolde*.
W.S. GILBERT

Franz Liszt … had a stock reply for young women who demanded unmerited praise of their singing. 'Maestro,' a young woman would enquire, 'do you think I have a good voice?' 'Ah, my dear young lady,' Liszt would reply, 'good is not the word for it.'
HERBERT PROCHNOW
*It Gives Me Great Pleasure*

Acting is very, very important in opera. But, of course, it is just as well if you also have a voice.
TITO GOBBI

I sometimes wonder which would be nicer – an opera without an interval, or an interval without an opera.
ERNEST NEWMAN

How wonderful operas would be if only there were no singers!
GIUSEPPE VERDI

Nobody really sings in an opera. They just make loud noise.
AMENITA GALLI-CURCI

In the closing scene of Wagner's *Lohengrin*, Slezak had sung his Farewell, and was about to make his departure in the boat drawn by a swan. The boat moved away before Slezak could step on board. He glanced at the audience. 'Tell me,' he said, 'what time is the next swan?'

There is a childlike, unsophisticated quality about opera which commands respect in this wicked world. All that hooting and hollering because somebody has pinched somebody else's girl, or killed the wrong man, or sold his soul to the devil. These are commonplaces in daily life ... and it is astonishing to hear them treated with so much noisy consideration.
ROBERTSON DAVIES
*The Table Talk of Samuel Marchbanks*

The opera is like a husband with a foreign title – expensive to support, hard to understand and therefore a supreme social challenge.
CLEVELAND AMORY

The Italians, truly, are eternal children. They paid infinitely more attention to the ballet than to the opera, and followed with breathless attention, and an air of the most serious credulity, the interminable adventures of a danseuse who went through every possible alteration of human experience on the points of her toes. The more I see of them the more struck I am with their having no sense of the ridiculous.

> HENRY JAMES
> in a letter to Fanny Kemble, 24 March 1881

Sleep is an excellent way of listening to an opera.

> JAMES STEPHENS

People are wrong when they say that opera is not what it used to be. It *is* what it used to be. That is what is wrong with it.

> NOEL COWARD

In Vienna ... everybody was too busy waltzing to bother about anything else. The Dances used to last from ten at night until seven in the morning ... It got to the point where some ballrooms had special chambers where expectant mothers could give birth after indulging in one last dance ... Other ballrooms had special chambers where indulgent young ladies could become expectant mothers.

> VICTOR BORGE
> My *Favourite Intervals*

I think the day of Oratorios is gone, like the day of painting Holy Families, etc.

> EDWARD FITZGERALD
> in a letter to F. Tennyson, 5 May 1848

"A popular song from M.r Nokes"

It should be 'The Lost Progression', for the young lady was mistaken in supposing she had ever heard any single chord 'like the sound of a great Amen'. Unless we are to suppose that she had already found the chord of C major for the final syllable of the word and was seeking the chord for the first syllable ... Fancy being in the room with her while she was strumming about and hunting after her chord! Fancy being in heaven with her when she had found it!

> SAMUEL BUTLER
> *Note-Books*

What makes the difference between an opera of Mozart's and the singing of a thrush in a wooden cage at the corner of the street? The one is nature, and the other is art: the one is paid for, and the other is not.

> WILLIAM HAZLITT
> 'The Opera', *Essays*

'This *must* be the music,' said he, 'of the Spears, for I'm curst if each note of it doesn't run through me.'

> THOMAS MOORE
> *The Fudge Family*

Joachim scraped away frantically making a sound after which an attempt to grate a nut effectively on a boot sole would have been as the strain of an Aeolian harp. The notes which were musical enough to have any discernible pitch at all were mostly out of tune. It was horrible – damnable! Had he been an unknown player ... he would not have escaped with his life.

> CORNO DE BASSETO, alias Bernard Shaw
> *London Music*, 1888/89

During the 1939–45 War the Polish pianist Pouisnoff gave a Chopin matinée recital in Newcastle-upon-Tyne in aid of a wartime charity. After the last encore, the Mayor appeared on the platform, resplendent in civic chain. 'I want to thank the Halls Committee for making available these premises,' he said. 'I want to thank the caretaker who opened them up for us; the cleaners who came in specially to clean them; the printers who donated the programmes; the many local firms who took advertising space in them; the young people who came in to sell them to us; and, last but not least, the artiste at the pian-er, Mr Pushinoff.'

> MAURICE LINDSAY, a very young officer-member of the audience

A famous String Quartet gave a highly successful concert in a north-country town. Afterwards, the Mayor made a speech. 'You might think we know nowt about music in these parts,' he explained. 'But we've enjoyed t'concert. We 'ope you'll come back, and that next time you'll bring the full band.'

At a concert in Carlisle, the pianist Peter Katin, having played a Rachmaninov piano concerto, was relaxing in the Green Room, while the orchestra continued the concert with Dvorak's New World Symphony. The Mayor, bored with the music, wandered into the Green Room. 'Why aren't you out there playing with the others?', he asked. 'There isn't a part in the New World Symphony for the piano,' Katin replied. The Mayor thought for a moment. 'Then you'll be paid less than the others?' he opined.

> PETER KATIN to Maurice Lindsay, 1963

You are quite right to prefer dogs – they are more entertaining than concert artists and cows, more prepossessing than great prima donnas.

> CLAUDE DEBUSSY
> in a letter to Jacques Durrand

Tchaikovsky thought of committing suicide for fear of being discovered a homosexual, but today, if you are a composer and not a homosexual, you might as well put a bullet through your head.

SERGEI DIAGHILEV

A teenage girl was talking to a friend about a new pop singer she had heard. 'I know he's going to be good,' she asserted. 'My father can't stand him.'

HERBERT PROCHNOW
*It Gives Me Great Pleasure*

We had a long dramatic recitative which went something like this – 'What's this I hear? The cheque with which you were to have paid for twenty-five thousand acres of lumber at a dollar an acre has not materialised? Then my previous option holds good. What have you to say to that?'

What I have to say is that the composers of *Jeptha*, *Don Giovanni*, and *Saint Paul*, putting their heads together, could not have coped with these words.... The Piece abounded in gems of unconscious humour, as when the hero turned to a number of guests at a Montreal evening party and bade them:

'Prate not to me
Of the open sea!'

JAMES AGATE
on *Lumber Love*, an opera by B. and E. Adams, 1938

Agnus Dei was a woman composer famous for her chirch music.

a schoolchild's exam answer

I have often wondered whether I have a taste for music or not. My ear appears to me as dull as my voice is incapable of

musical expression, and yet I feel the utmost pleasure in any
such music as I can comprehend ... I have a reasonable good
ear for a jig, but your solos and sonatas give me the spleen.
SIR WALTER SCOTT
*Journal*, 30 July 1827

To know whether you are enjoying a piece of music or not
you must see whether you find yourself looking at the
advertisements for Pears' soap at the end of the programme.
SAMUEL BUTLER
*Note-Books*

You must observe, my friend, that it is the custom of this
country, when a lady or a gentleman happens to sing, for
the company to sit as mute and motionless as statues. Every
feature, every limb, must seem to correspond in fixed
attention; and while the song continues they are to remain
in a state of universal petrification.
OLIVER GOLDSMITH
*The Citizen of the World*, 1762

Musical people are so absurdly unreasonable. They always
want one to be perfectly dumb at the very moment when
one is longing to be absolutely deaf.
OSCAR WILDE
*An Ideal Husband*, 1895

Music makes one feel so romantic – at least it always gets on
one's nerves – which is the same thing nowadays.
OSCAR WILDE
*A Woman of No Importance*, 1893

An unalterable and unquestioned law of the musical world
required that the German text of French operas sung by

Swedish artists should be translated into Italian for the clearer understanding of English-speaking audiences.

> EDITH WHARTON
> *The Age of Innocence*, 1920

Of course the music is a great difficulty. You see, if one plays good music people don't listen and if one plays bad music people don't talk.

> OSCAR WILDE
> *The Importance of Being Earnest*

It sounds as if it were telling you something, but does it tell you anything? This music. It gets excited and joyous, for no reason, just as you get excited and joyous in dreams; it's sad and tender – about nothing ... Your mind runs along according to the rhythm. But all to no effect. It doesn't give you anything real. It doesn't let you out.

> H.G. WELLS
> *The Autocracy of Mr Parham*

What the English like is something they can beat time to, something that hits them straight on the drum of the ear.

> GEORGE FREDERICK HANDEL
> quoted in Schmid, *C.W. von Gluck*, 1854

I have no ear ... Organically, I am incapable of a tune. I have been practising 'God Save the King' all my life; whistling and humming of it over to myself in solitary corners: and am not yet arrived, they tell me, within many quavers of it.

> CHARLES LAMB
> 'A Chapter on Ears', *Essays of Elia*

We were none of us musical, though Miss Jenkins beat time, out of time, by way of appearing to be so.
ELIZABETH GASKELL
*Cranford*

Though there seemed no chance of [Catherine] throwing a whole party into raptures by a prelude on the pianoforte of her own composition, she could listen to other people's performance with very little fatigue.
JANE AUSTEN
*Northanger Abbey*

There are few people in England, I suppose, who have more true enjoyment of music than myself, or a better natural taste. If I had ever learnt, I should have been a great proficient. And so would Anne, if her health had allowed her to apply.
JANE AUSTEN
*Pride and Prejudice*

My wife is a great Pretender to Musick, and very ignorant of it; but far gone in the Italian taste.
RICHARD STEELE
*Spectator*, 2nd November 1711

O! sir, I must not tell you my age. They say woman and music should never be dated.
OLIVER GOLDSMITH
*She Stoops to Conquer*

Some to church repair
Not for the doctrine but the music there.
ALEXANDER POPE
*Essay on Criticism*

A pianist, who was also a keen golfer, was giving a recital in London. Two fellow musicians met. Said one: 'I hear So-and-So is playing Beethoven to-night.' 'Oh, is he?' said the other. 'I'm afraid Beethoven is going to lose.'

I have often protested against the habit of digesting Beethoven with the aid of a diet of Carlyle's *French Revolution* relieved by doses of *The Scarlet Pimpernel*.

    SIR DONALD FRANCIS TOVEY
    *Essays in Musical Analysis*

A man came to Cherubini with a score said to be by Méhul. After examining it, Cherubini said: 'It is not by Méhul. It is too bad to be his.'

    'Will you believe me, M. Cherubini, if I tell you it is mine?' said the visitor.

    'No,' replied Cherubini. 'It is too good to be yours.'

    F.J. CROWEST
    *Cherubini*, 1926

It is not unjust to define amateur concerts by saying that the music performed at them seems to have been composed to make those who render it happy and drive those who listen to despair.

    ADOLPHE ADAM
    *Souvenirs d'un Musicien*

During the playing of Rossini's 'William Tell' overture at the Albert Hall, an American lady said: 'Back home, this is known as "The Lone Ranger".'

    PETERBOROUGH
    *Daily Telegraph*, 13 July 1979

The great violinist Fritz Kreisler was strolling with a friend in a New York street when they passed a fish shop. Kreisler waved a hand towards the rows of protruding eyes and gaping mouths on the slab.

'Ah,' he said. 'That reminds me – I have a concert tonight.'

Carmen is a cigar-makeress from a tabago factory who loves with Don José of the mounting guard. Carmen takes a flower from her corsets and lances it to Don José (Duet: 'Talk me of my mother'). There is a noise inside the tabaga factory and the revolting cigar-makeresses burst into the stage. Carmen is arrested and Don José is ordered to mounting guard, but Carmen seduces him and he lets her escape.

Act 2. The Tavern. Carmen, Frasquita, Mercedes, Zuniga, Morales. Carmen's aria ('the sistrums are tinkling'). Enter Escamillio, a balls-fighter. Enter the smugglers (Duet: 'We have in mind a business') but Carmen refuses to penetrate because Don José has liberated from prison. He just now arrives (Aria: 'Slop, here who comes!') but hear are the bugles singing his retreat. Don José will leave and draws his sword. Called by Carmen shreiks, the two smugglers interfere with her but Don José is bound to dessert, he will follow into them ...

Act 4 a place in Saville. Procession of Balls-fighters, the roaring of the balls heard in the arena. Escamillio enters (Aria and chorus: 'Toreador, toreador. All hail the balls of a Toreador!'). Enter Don José (Aria: 'I do not threaten, I besooch you') but Carmen repels him wants to join with Escamillio now chaired by the crowd. Don José stabs her (Aria: 'Oh rupture, rupture, you may arrest me, I did kill der') he sings 'Oh my beautiful Carmen, my subductive Carmen ...

> JOHN JULIUS NORWICH
> a French opera-house programme note reprinted in *A Christmas Cracker*

It cannot be too often pointed out that ... the programme writer has no business to say anything that interferes with the listener's enjoyment of the music.

> SIR DONALD FRANCIS TOVEY
> *Essays in Musical Analysis*

When preparations were afoot for the annual Gaelic Mod, or singing contest, organized by the Gaelic Society of London, the President remarked that one group of singers would be singing in Gaelic for the first time and that ninety per cent of another group had never seen Scotland.

'But what has all this to do with the English?' someone asked. 'Everything,' he replied. 'They give the prizes.'

I find it very healthy if an audience reacts in any way.
> GARY BERTINI, Israeli conductor
> after an audience slow-clapped a modern work, 1969


Yes ... Barbirolli has worked wonders with the Hallé. He has transformed it into the finest chamber orchestra in the country.
> SIR THOMAS BEECHAM


After Beecham had given a performance of a Mozart opera in New York, conductor Fritz Reiner, who had been in the audience, went round to congratulate him.

'Thank you for a delightful evening with Beecham and Mozart.'

'Why drag in Mozart?' murmured Sir Thomas.
> LESLIE AYRES
> *The Wit of Music*


Beethoven could hardly put out the version of his opera [*Fidelio*] with the same old overture, so he wrote a third one, better than the first and longer than the second. It's the one containing the famous off-stage trumpet call ... Leopold Stokowski ... was conducting the Philadelphia Orchestra in the Leonora No 3 Overture, and both times the off-stage call didn't sound on cue. As soon as the performance ended, Stokowski rushed into the wings, ready to give the delinquent trumpet-player a tongue-lashing, when he found the fellow struggling in the arms of a burly watchman. 'I tell you, you can't play that damned thing in here,' the watchman was saying, 'there's a concert going on.'
> VICTOR BORGE
> *My Favourite Intervals*

He (an English conductor) always stands with his legs together while conducting. You cannot *conduct* if you always stand with your legs together. It is physically impossible.

ARNOLD BENNETT
quoted in *Things that have Interested Me*

Why do we have to have all these third-rate foreign conductors around, when we have so many second-rate ones of our own?

SIR THOMAS BEECHAM

Sir Thomas Beecham was travelling in the no-smoking carriage of a train when a woman passenger lit a cigarette with the words 'You won't object if I smoke?' To which Beecham replied, 'Certainly not – and you won't object if I'm sick.'

'I don't think you know who I am,' the woman angrily

pointed out. 'I am one of the director's wives.' To which Beecham riposted, 'Madam, if you were the director's only wife, I should still be sick.'

quoted in *Quote ... Unquote*, edited by Nigel Rees

While rehearsing for a performance of *Messiah*, Beecham stopped the proceedings and addressed the choir.

'When we sing "All we like sheep have gone astray", might we, please, have a little more regret and a little less satisfaction?'

Sir Thomas Beecham was rehearsing the Triumphal Scene from Verdi's *Aida*. He made the chorus repeat one section over and over again, during which one of the trained horses forgot its training. Sir Thomas stopped the rehearsal, glowered at the offending horse, and exclaimed, 'Disgusting spectacle, but gad, what a critic!'

'Have you heard any Stockhausen?' Sir Thomas Beecham was asked. 'No,' he replied, 'but I believe I have trodden in some.'

Too much counterpoint; what is worse, Protestant counterpoint.
> SIR THOMAS BEECHAM
> quoted by Neville Cardus,
> *The Guardian*, 8 March 1971

A trombone player made his debut one morning. 'You are new, aren't you?' asked Beecham. 'What's your name?'
'Ball, sir.'
'How very singular,' observed Sir Thomas.

A woman confided to Sir Thomas that her son wanted to learn an instrument, but she couldn't bear the purgatory of his practising in the initial stages. 'What is the best instrument?' she asked. 'I have no hesitation, madam,' he said, 'in saying the bagpipes. They sound exactly the same when you have finished learning them as when you started learning them.'

   *Beecham Stories*, ed. Atkins and Newman

[Beecham] was rehearsing an aria by Mozart with a young and not very experienced soprano. The young woman got a fraction ahead of the orchestra ... but in spite of the conductor's quizzical looks and the obvious discomfort of the orchestra, she proceeded calmly on her way. At last Sir Thomas stopped the players and leaning down from the rostrum said to her, 'My dear young lady, I think I should tell you that you are being *followed!*'

   ALEC ROBERTSON
   *More than Music*

Even Beethoven thumped the tub; the Ninth Symphony was composed by a kind of Mr Gladstone of music.

SIR THOMAS BEECHAM
quoted in *Beecham Stories*, eds. Atkins and Newman

Méhul is one of those composers whose fate is to be overrated by historians and underrated by musicians who approach his music keyed up to its historical reputation ... His chief misfortune is that his field of musical activity was opera ... He is said to have written forty-two operas, of which I have read fifteen. Sir Thomas Beecham, when I mentioned the subject to him some years ago, had read about twice as many, and probably by this time knows all the rest by heart.

SIR DONALD FRANCIS TOVEY
note on Méhul's Overture, *Le Jeune Sage et le Vieux Fou*

'I hear you have been staying at Lord So-and-So's,' a friend said to Beecham.

'Yes,' Sir Thomas replied, 'I spent a month down there last weekend.'

At a birthday dinner for Beecham, the chairman read congratulatory telegrams from leading musical figures from all over the world. There was tremendous applause. As it died away, Beecham took his cigar from his mouth and said, 'What? Nothing from Mozart?'

During a break in rehearsal, a photographer asked Sir Thomas Beecham if he could appear to be conducting while a picture was taken.

'My dear fellow,' said Sir Thomas, 'I never *appear* to be conducting. Either I conduct, or I do not conduct.'

When shown an inscription in a Sussex graveyard which read: Here lies a fine musician and a great organist, Sir Thomas remarked 'How on earth did they get them both into so small a grave?'

A musicologist is a man who can read music but can't hear it.

> SIR THOMAS BEECHAM
> quoted by H. Proctor-Greig in *Beecham Remembered*

In the days when Sir Malcolm Sargent was the cultural pride of Liverpool, Sir Thomas Beecham turned up at the leading city hotel and asked to have the best suite. 'I'm sorry sir,' he was told, 'it's already been taken.' 'Then move whoever is in it elsewhere,' Sir Thomas demanded. 'I'm sorry, sir, that can't be done,' said the receptionist. 'I don't think you know who I am,' declared Beecham majestically. 'I am Sir Thomas Beecham.' 'I'm sorry, sir,' replied the receptionist, 'but I still couldn't let you have it, not even if you were Sir Malcolm Sargent.'

My dear fellow, I had no idea the Chinese were so musical.

> SIR THOMAS BEECHAM
> on hearing a rumour that Sir Malcolm Sargent had been kidnapped in China

After a rousing performance of *Rule Britannia*, King George VI said to Sir Malcolm Sargent, 'You will in future always include that in the programme when I am present.'

'But, Your Majesty, how can I include *Rule Britannia* if I am about to conduct a sacred work like the *St Matthew Passion?*

'No problem. I shall not be there.'

> quoted by Kenneth Rose in *Kings, Queens and Courtiers*

I don't enjoy being Malcolm Sargent.
  SIR MALCOLM SARGENT

A French composer and conductor who was rehearsing a difficult modern work of his own with a British orchestra wasn't satisfied with the way a certain woodwind passage was being interpreted.

'No, no,' he said irritably, 'not like that, like this ...' And he sang: 'La-la ... lalala ... laaa, la, la.'

'Ah,' said the musician, also singing, 'You mean, la-la ... lalala ... laaa, la, la?'

'Yes,' beamed the conductor, 'that's it!'

'Good,' said the clarinettist. 'Now we have established we can both sing it, who's going to play it?'
  ROBIN RAY
  *Preview*

When I am with composers, I say I am a conductor. When I am with conductors, I say I am a composer.
  LEONARD BERNSTEIN
  *The World in Vogue*

I never use a score when conducting my orchestra ... Does a lion tamer enter a cage with a book on how to tame a lion?
> DIMITRI MITROPOULOS, 22 January 1951

While the famous Corelli, at Rome, was playing some musical composition of his own to a select company in the private apartment of his patron, a Cardinal, he observed in the height of his harmony that his eminence was engaged in a detach'd conversation; upon which he suddenly stopt short and gently laid down his instrument. The Cardinal, surprised, at the unexpected cessation, asked him if a string was broke. To which Corelli, in an honest consciousness of what was due to his musick, replied, 'No, sir, I was only afraid I interrupted business.'
> COLLEY CIBBER
> *An Apology for his Life*, 1740

There is one god – Bach – and Mendelssohn is his prophet.
> HECTOR BERLIOZ

Bach almost persuades me to be a Christian.
> ROGER FRY
> quoted by Virginia Wolf in *Roger Fry*

I don't know how, with no vibrato, Bach could have so many sons.
> PAUL HINDEMITH
> quoted by Jacobson in *Reverberations*

A tub of pork and beer.
> HECTOR BERLIOZ on Handel

A good old pagan at heart.
> EDWARD FITZGERALD on Handel

Bach and his family

He is the master of us all.
JOSEPH HAYDN, on hearing the 'Hallelujah Chorus'

Handel is only fourth rate. He is not even interesting.
PIOTR ILYICH TCHAIKOVSKY

George Frederick Handel

Whoever studies music, let his daily bread be Haydn. Beethoven, indeed, is admirable, he is incomparable, but he has not the same usefulness as Haydn. He is not a necessity.
JEAN INGRES

Both Gluck and Mozart are unintelligible as opera writers until we realise that their points of view converge to much the same result. Both of them were supreme masters in the art of bullying their librettists; in fact greater masters than Wagner, who was sometimes a little shy of bullying himself.

    SIR DONALD FRANCIS TOVEY
    *Essays in Musical Analysis*

This boy [the fifteen-year-old Mozart] will cause us all to be forgotten.

    JOHANN ADOLPH HASSE, 1761

Wolfgang Amadeus Mozart

Of all composers, Mozart probably has shown the greatest ingenuity in marrying music and words ... This witty alliance of musician and poet ... gives a kind of pleasure – but a pleasure that originates in the mind, and ... does not belong to the marvellous sphere of the arts.

GERMAINE DE STAËL
*De l'Allemagne*

Since he was a little on the lazy side, Mozart didn't start writing operas until he was twelve.

VICTOR BORGE
My *Favourite Intervals*

I write as a sow piddles.

WOLFGANG AMADEUS MOZART

It was just as I expected; no money, only a gold watch. I now have five watches, and am seriously thinking of having an additional watch pocket sewn on each leg of my trousers, so that when I visit some great lord, it will not occur to him to present me with another.

WOLFGANG AMADEUS MOZART
in a letter in 1777

I could not compose operas like *Don Giovanni* and *Figaro*. I hold them in aversion. They are too frivolous for me.

LUDWIG VAN BEETHOVEN
*Impressions by Contemporaries*

He [Beethoven] tried to think in music, almost to reason in music; whereas perhaps we should be contented with feeling in it. It can never speak very definitely ...

EDWARD FITZGERALD
in a letter to F. Tennyson, 31 March 1842

'Ah! that is what costs so much money!' said Madam Crémière to Madame Massin …

'Heaven preserve me from spending so much money to let my little Aline make a hubbub of this sort about the house!' replied Madame Massin.

'She says it is by *Beethoven*, who after all is said to be a great musician', said the surveyor. 'He has a certain reputation.'

'Well, he is not going to have one at Nemours,' rejoined Madame Crémière. 'He has the right name – *Bête à vent.*'

HONORÉ DE BALZAC
*Ursule Mirouët*

Ludwig van Beethoven

Beethoven always sounds to me like the upsetting of a bag of nails, with here and there also a dropped hammer.

JOHN RUSHKIN
letter in 1881

It will be generally admitted that Beethoven's Fifth Symphony is the most sublime noise that has ever penetrated into the ear of Man.

E.M. FOSTER
*Howard's End*

I freely confess that I have never been able to enjoy these last works of Beethoven. Yes, I must even include the much-admired Ninth Symphony among them, the first three movements of which, in spite of some isolated flashes of genius, are to my mind inferior to all the eight previous symphonies. The fourth movement is in my opinion so monstrous and tasteless, so trivial in its grasp of Schiller's Ode, that I can never bring myself to understand how a genius like Beethoven could have written it.

LOUIS SPOHR
*Autobiography*

Then came Schubert's 'Erl König', which I daresay, is very fine but with which I have absolutely nothing in common.

SAMUEL BUTLER
*Notebooks*

Some cry up Haydn, some Mozart,
Just as the whim bites; for my part
I do not give a farthing candle
For either of them, or for Handel –
Cannot a man live free and easy
Without admiring Pergolesi?

Or through the world with comfort go
That never heard of Dr Blow? ...
The devil with his foot so cloven
For ought I care may take Beethoven
And, if the bargain does not suit
I'll throw Weber in to boot ...
    CHARLES LAMB


I composed the overture to *Otello* in a little room in the Barbaja Palace wherein the baldest and fiercest of directors had forcibly locked me with a lone plate of spaghetti and the threat that I would not be allowed to leave the room alive until I had written the last note.

I wrote the overture to *La Gazze Ladra* the day of its opening in the theatre itself, where I was imprisoned by the director and under the surveillance of four stagehands who were instructed to throw my original text through the window, page by page, to the copyists waiting below to transcribe it. In default of pages, they were ordered to throw me out of the window bodily. I did better with *The Barber*. I did not compose an overture, but selected for it one called *Elisabeth*. The public was completely satisfied.
    GIOACCHINO ROSSINI
    *Letter to an Unknown Composer*


Rossini wrote the first and last acts of *William Tell*. God wrote the second act.
    GAETANO DONIZETTI


When Donizetti heard that Rossini had completed the whole of *The Barber of Seville* in three weeks, he shook his head. 'Yes, yes,' he cried. 'Rossini always was a lazy fellow.'

Rossini was sitting among a group of friends, when his manservant announced that a well-known tenor was asking to see him. 'Certainly,' said Rossini. 'But please ask him to leave his top note outside with his hat and stick. He may of course collect it again as he leaves.'

Give me a laundry list and I'll set it to music.
GIOACCHINO ROSSINI

Rossini

How wonderful opera would be if there were no singers.
GIOACCHINO ROSSINI

One cannot judge *Lohengrin* from a first hearing, and I certainly do not intend to hear it a second time.
GIOACCHINO ROSSINI

On his 70th birthday Rossini's friends collected twenty thousand francs to erect a monument. 'What a waste of money,' the composer groaned. 'Give me the cash, and I'll stand on the pedestal myself.'
>VICTOR BORGE
>*My Favourite Intervals*

Rossini, in music, is the genius of sheer animal spirits. It is a species as inferior to that of Mozart, as the cleverness of a smart boy is to that of a man of sentiment; but it is genius nevertheless.
>LEIGH HUNT
>*Going to the Play Again*, 1828

Hats off, gentlemen – a genius!
>ROBERT SCHUMANN
>reviewing Chopin's Opus 2 in the *Allgemeine Musikalische Zeitung*, 1831

Play Mozart in memory of me.
>FRÉDÉRIC CHOPIN – his last words

The saying, 'I have thrown it into the fire,' is an example of shameless modesty ... I detest people who throw their compositions into the fire!'
>ROBERT SCHUMANN
>*On Music and Musicians*

Mr Ernest Newman
Said: Next week Schumann,
But when next week came
It was Wagner just the same.
>ANON.

I ... went once to the pit of the Covent Garden Italian Opera to hear Meyerbeer's *Huguenots* ... But the first act was so noisy, and ugly, that I came away ... Meyerbeer is a man of genius ... but he has scarce any melody, and is rather grotesque and noisy than really powerful.

>    EDWARD FITZGERALD
>    in a letter to F. Tennyson, 8 June 1852

Meyerbeer's music, as a witty woman once remarked to me, is like stage scenery – it should not be scrutinised too closely.

>    CAMILLE SAINT-SAËNS
>    *Musical Memories*

Berlioz is a regular freak without a vestige of talent.

>    FELIX MENDELSSOHN
>    in a letter, 1831

He was dying all his life.

>    HECTOR BERLIOZ on Chopin

Once dead, he will live for a long time.

>    STEPHEN HALLÉ on Berlioz, 1844

Paganini ... will make a fortune because he can actually sell the tones of his fiddle at so much a scrape.

>    SAMUEL TAYLOR COLERIDGE
>    *Table Talk*

His [Mendelssohn's] talent is enormous, extraordinary prodigious. I am not open to a charge of partisanship in saying this, because he told me frankly that he could not understand my music.

>    HECTOR BERLIOZ
>    letter to Ferdinand Hiller, 17 September 1831

With what you say of Berlioz's overture I thoroughly agree. It is a chaotic, prosaic piece, and yet more humanly conceived than some of his others ... His orchestration is such a frightful muddle, such an incongruous mess that one ought to wash one's hands after handling one of his scores.

> FELIX MENDELSSOHN
> in a letter to Ignaz Moscheles, April 1834

In order to succeed today you have to be either dead or German.

> GEORGES BIZET
> in a letter to Louis Gallet

Played Brahms. It irritates me that this self-conscious mediocrity should be recognised as a genius. In comparison with him, Raff was a giant, not to speak of Rubenstein who was a much greater man.

> PIOTR ILYICH TCHAIKOVSKY
> in a letter to Nadejda von Mech, 7/19 October 1880

Too much beer and beard.

> PAUL DUKAS of Brahms
> quoted in Demuth, *Vincent D'Indy*

I have played over the music of that scoundrel Brahms. What a giftless bastard!

> PIOTR ILYICH TCHAIKOVSKY
> *Diary*, 1886

I once sent him a song and asked him to make a cross wherever he thought it was faulty. Brahms returned it untouched, saying, 'I don't want to make a cemetery of your composition.'

> HUGO WOLF

A 1905 drawing of Joachim

Brahms is a competent musician who knows his counterpoint and has sometimes good, occasionally excellent, sometimes bad, now and again already familiar ideas, and often none at all.

> HUGO WOLF
> *Collected Criticism*, 30 November 1884

A young composer came to Brahms and asked if he might play for the master a funeral march he had composed in memory of Beethoven. Well, permission was granted, and

A contemporary caricature showing Dr Hanslick, the bitter critic of Wagner, burning incense before a statue of Brahms

the young man earnestly played away. When he was through, he sought Brahms's opinion. 'I tell you,' said the great man candidly. 'I'd be much happier if you were dead, and Beethoven had written the march.
> ANDRE PRÉVIN
> *Music Face to Face*

I have composed too much.
> ANTONIN DVORAK
> in a letter to Sibelius

You do write a bit hastily.
> JOHANNES BRAHMS
> in a letter to Dvorak

Symphonic boaconstrictors.
> JOHANNES BRAHMS on Bruckner's symphonies
> quoted in Specht, *Johannes Brahms*

A swindle that will be forgotten in a few years.
> JOHANNES BRAHMS on Bruckner's symphonies
> quoted in Watson, *Brahms*

At a concert where one of (Debussy's) works was in the programme, I asked Rimsky-Korsakov what he thought of it. He replied ... 'Better not listen to it; you risk getting used to it, and then you would end up liking it.'
> IGOR STRAVINSKY
> *Chroniques de ma Vie*

One has in one's mouth the bizarre and charming taste of a pink bonbon stuffed with snow.
> CLAUDE DEBUSSY on Grieg
> in a letter to H.T. Finck, 1905

I am sure my music has a taste of codfish in it.
>      EDUARD GRIEG
>      in a speech in 1903

Of course there are splendid things in Wagner. But he
would go on so. He needed a good sub-editor.
>      CONSTANT LAMBERT

After silence that which comes nearest to expressing the
inexpressible is music ... Compared with Beethoven's or
Mozart's, the ceaseless torrent of Wagner's music is very
poor in silence. Perhaps that is one reason why it seems so
much less significant than theirs. It says less because it is
always speaking.
>      ALDOUS HUXLEY
>      *Music at Night*

Wagner has good moments, but bad quarter-hours.
>      GIOACCHINO ROSSINI
>      quoted in *Wagnerism, a Protest* by Major H.W.L.
>      Hime, 1884

That old poisoner.
>      CLAUDE DEBUSSY on Wagner
>      letter to Pierre Louys, 1890

Richard Wagner was a musician who wrote music which is
better than it sounds.
>      MARK TWAIN

I like Wagner's music better than anybody's. It is so loud
that one can talk the whole time.
>      OSCAR WILDE
>      *The Picture of Dorian Gray*, 1891

Richard Wagner

Wagner is the Puccini of music.
attributed to J.B. MORTON

Is Wagner a human being at all? Is he not rather a disease?
FRIEDRICH NIETZSCHE
*Der Fall Wagner*, 1888

74

When Verdi was asked by journalists if he, like Wagner, had a theory about the theatre, Verdi replied, 'Yes. The theatre should be full.'

ANON.

It was a pity I wrote *Cavalleria* first. I was crowned before I was king.

PIETRO MASCAGNI to Puccini

What I'd like best of all, time and again, would be to set myself to music.

RICHARD STRAUSS
in a letter to Hugo von Hoffmannsthal

If there were a conservatory in Hell, and if one of its talented students was to compose a symphony based on the study of the Seven Plagues of Egypt, and if he had written one similar to Rachmaninoff's, he would have brilliantly accomplished his task and would have delighted the inhabitants of Hell.

CESAR CUI
*St Petersburg News*, March 1897

I have always found it difficult to study. I have learnt almost entirely what I have learnt by trying it on the dog.

RALPH VAUGHAN WILLIAMS
quoted by Trend, *The Music Makers*

A student at Cornell University who played Vaughan Williams a movement from his own dissonant quartet on the piano provoked the observation: 'If a tune should occur to you, my boy, don't hesitate to write it down.'

quoted by Trend, *The Music Makers*

Almost all the British composers who have achieved anything have studied at home and only gone abroad when they were mature – Elgar, Holst, Parry, Bax, Walton. Stanford is an exception, but he was by no means a beginner when he went to study abroad and as a matter of fact he never quite recovered from Leipzig. On the other hand, I have known many young composers with a genuine native invention who have gone to Germany or France in their most impressionable years and have come back speaking a musical language which can only be described as broken French or German. They have had their native qualities swamped and never recovered their personality.

    RALPH VAUGHAN WILLIAMS
    in a letter to Lord Kennet, 1941


I am gradually beginning to feel like a cornerstone on which every passerby can pass the water of his artistic opinion.

    PAUL HINDEMITH
    in a letter to Willy Strecke, 1946


Gustav Holst, who aimed so much at austerity in his last years, can surely not have been offended when a work of his (the Fugal Concerto) was described as the 'Frugal Concerto', and he was surely too generous to mind if some of the praise was transferred to the performers when it was said that he had written excellent ballet music for the 'Perfect Foot'.

    ERIC BLOM
    *A Musical Postbag*, 1940


Never compose anything unless the not composing of it becomes a positive nuisance to you.

    GUSTAV HOLST
    in a letter to W.G. Whittaker, 1921

John Ireland always felt that his music was not accorded its due in the matter of performance. He was particularly resentful that he had never received the broadcasting accolade of being the BBC 'Composer of the Week'. When at last the BBC did accord him this honour, it was found that there were not enough recordings of his music to fill the daily slot. He therefore shared the week's programmes with Gustav Holst. Meeting Ireland soon after, a friend said, 'Well, John. You'll be pleased that at last they've made you Composer of the Week.' 'Yes,' Ireland replied. 'It was very good. But I didn't much like the upholstery.'

 JULIAN HERBAGE
 (dedicatee of Ireland's *London Overture*) to Maurice
 Lindsay

That critics should be honest we have the right to demand, and critical dishonesty we are bound to expose. If the writer will tell us what he thinks, though his thoughts be absolutely vague and useless, we can forgive him; but when he tells us what he does not think, actuated either by friendship or by animosity, then there should be no pardon for him.

 ANTHONY TROLLOPE
 *An Autobiography*

Bach is a Colossus of Rhodes, beneath whom all musicians pass and will continue to pass. Mozart is the most beautiful, Rossini the most brilliant, but Bach is the most comprehensive: he has said all there is to say.

 CHARLES GOUNOD
 *Le Figaro*, 19 October 1891

Though full of great musical lore
Old Bach is a terrible bore.

A fugue without tune
He thought was a boon,
So he wrote seventeen thousand or more.
    *Musical Herald*, 1884

Some say, compared with Bononcini,
That Mynheer Handel's but a ninny;
Others aver that he to Handel
Is scarcely fit to hold a candle;
Strange all this difference should be
'Twixt Tweedledum and Tweedledee!
    JOHN BYROM

The programme book for a festival performance of *Acis and
Galathea* ... on the day of the concert was perceived with
horror by the whole diocese to contain the ... line: 'O
ruddier than the clergy'.
    ERIC BLOM
    *A Musical Postbag*, 1940

I think the Hallujah Chorus might be improved by steeping
in boiling water for ten minutes or so.
    BERNARD SHAW
    *Mrs Patrick Campbell Correspondence*

If I had the power I would insist on all oratorios being sung
in the costume of the period – with the possible exception
of *The Creation*.
    SIR ERNEST NEWMAN
    *New York Post*, 1924

Nobody will fail to see in Mozart a man of talent and an
experienced, abundant and agreeable composer. But I have
as yet encountered no thorough connoisseur of art who

took him for a correct ... artist ... Least of all will tasteful criticism regard him in the matter of poetry, as a true and sensitive composer.

*Musikalische Monatschrift*, 1793

*Emperor Joseph II*: 'Very many notes, my dear Mozart.'
*Mozart*: 'Exactly the necessary number, Your Majesty.'
    after the première of *Die Entführung aus dem Serail*,
    1782

There was a young lady named Cager
Who, as the result of a wager,
Consented to fart
The whole oboe part
Of Mozart's Quartet in F major.
    ANON

I'll give another Kreutzer if they'll stop the thing.
    a voice from the gallery (reported by Carl Czerny)
    at the first performance of Beethoven's
    Eroica Symphony

Opinions are much divided concerning the merits of the Pastoral Symphony of Beethoven, though very few venture to deny that it is much too long.

*Harmonicum*, edited by William Ayrton, June 1823

Experts say that the Broadwood was not Beethoven's favourite make of piano. He apparently preferred the Austrian Graf. Had he played the Broadwood more, of course, it might not have been in such good condition after its recent restoration. Beethoven was a notorious thumper, especially when in a bad mood. On one celebrated occasion, performing a new concerto, he forgot he was the

soloist and began to conduct. At the first sforzando he waved his arms so violently that he knocked over the lights on the piano. He started the concerto again, this time with two choirboys holding the lights, but on reaching the same sforzando he hit one of the choirboys, who dropped his light, while the other was forced to duck. Beethoven became enraged by the audience's laughter, then when he struck the first chord six of the piano's strings broke.

> *Glasgow Herald* Editorial, 5 June 1992

Rossini never dogmatised; his approach to music was instinctive rather than intellectual. This is shown in his famous saying that there are only two kinds of music, the good and the bad; or that other, less known, where he states that every kind of music is good except the boring kind.

> FRANCIS TOYE
> *Rossini: A Study in Tragi-Comedy, 1934*

There was a composer called Spohr
Whose works were a hundred or mohr.
His great work *Jessonda*
Long time was a wonda,
But now his successes are o'hr.
    *Musical Herald*, 1888

Samuel Westley [sic] before he could write was a composer
and mentally set the airs of several oratorios, which he
retained in memory till he was eight years old, and then
wrote them down.
    DR CHARLES BURNEY
    *Paper in the Philophical Transactions of the Royal
    Society, 1779*

Ours are days when taste must be carefully watched, and the works of Dr Schumann (with some trifling exceptions) are too pretending to be endured.

H.F. CHORLEY
*The Athenaeum*, 1856

There is an excuse at present for Chopin's delinquencies; he is entrammelled in the enthralling bonds of that enchantress Georges Sand ... We wonder how she ... can be content to wanton away her dreamlike existence with an artistical nonentity like Chopin.

*Musical World*, London, October 1840

Meyerbeer is a fellow of not a solitary new idea, whose invention is a bath for commonplaces to swim about in ... as melodist, null, 'as harmonist, *nuller* still.

J.W. DAVIDSON
*The Examiner*, 1842

There was a J.W.D.
Who thought a composer to be.
But his muse wouldn't budge
So he set up as judge
Of better composers than he.
of J.W. Davison, chief music critic of *The Times*, 1848–78, quoted in Charles Reid, *The Music Monster*, 1984

There was a composer called Auber
Who seldom was sombre or Sauber.
Yet he held aloof
From the opera bouffe,
But he lived past life's golden October.
*Musical Herald*, 1888

It only irritated Brahms
To tickle him under the arms.
What really helped him to compose
Was to be stroked on the nose.
E.C. BENTLEY
*Biography for Beginners*

The Bach Choir gave a concert on the 16th. I was not present. There are some sacrifices which should not be demanded twice from any man, and one of them is listening to Brahms' Requiem.
BERNARD SHAW
*Music in London*, 1890–94

It is almost as old-fashioned to enjoy Brahms as to be thrilled by a Valentine; but then it is precisely the old-fashionedness of the enjoyment which people like.
ERIC BLOM
*A Musical Postbag*, 1940

To Dvorak's Requiem ... I could not be made to listen again, since the penalty of default did not exceed death ... It is hard to understand the frame of mind of an artist who at this time of day sits down to write a Requiem *à propos de bottes*. One can fancy an undertaker doing it readily enough; he would know as a matter of business that in music, as in joiner's work, you can take the poorest materials and set the public gaping at them by simply covering them with black cloth and coffin-nails. But why should a musician condescend to speculate thus in sensationalism and superstition?
BERNARD SHAW
*Music in London*, 1890–94

Tchaikovsky's piano trio in A minor was played in Vienna for the first time; the faces of the listeners almost expressed the wish that it should be the last time. It belongs to the category of suicidal compositions, which kill themselves by their meritless length.

EDUARD HANSLICK
*Am Ende des Jahrhunderts*, Berlin 1899

What do you think of Stainer's Crucifixion? A very good idea.

graffiti in the Royal College of Music

'My dear friends, before we start I ask your forgiveness, *in advance* for all the unpleasant things I shan't fail to say to you in a moment.'

JACQUES OFFENBACH, at the beginning of his rehearsals

A skeleton with pince-nez who looks as if he's raping a 'cello.

The GONCOURT BROTHERS on Offenbach (1858)

When it was daylight, a quaint figure wearing a white tie and big dark glasses strolled along the Boulevard des Capucins. It was Léonce the comedian who, as Pluto in *Orphée* had made audiences sick with laughter at his clowning. He went up to Number 8 and rang the bell.

'M. Offenbach is dead,' sighed the concierge. 'He died very gently, without realising it.'

'Ah,' replied Léonce gravely: 'how annoyed he'll be when he finds out.'

JAMES HARDING
*Jacques Offenbach: A Biography*

The Abbé Liszt
Hit the piano with his fist.
That was the way
He used to play.
     E.C. BENTLEY
     *Biography for Beginners*

While young, the unabashed Franz
Embarked on a Period Glanze.
His honour-sheathed swords,
Entangled in chords,
Nearly caused him his own Totentanz.
     BERNARD P. LANGLEY
     *Lisztrionics*

A German printer innocent of French had mistaken the
title of Bazzini's 'Ronde des lutins', for 'Ronde de crétins',
to which Liszt ... remarked that such a piece must have an
incalculably large audience.
     ERIC BLOM
     *A Musical Postbag*

Tchaikovsky's Violin Concerto poses for the first time the
appalling notion that there can be works of music that stink
to the ear.
     EDUARD HANSLICK, 1881

I like listening to Tchaikovsky's Fifth just as I like looking
at a fuschia drenched with rain.
     JAMES AGATE
     *Ego 8*, 1847

A vacuum has been described as nothing shut up in a box,
and the prelude entitled *L'Aprés-midi d'un faune* may aptly
be described as nothing expressed in musical terms.
     *Referee*, London, 1904

It would be impossible to conceive a finer vehicle of expression than that invented by Debussy through the simple yet original process of abolishing rhythm, melody and tonality from music and thus leaving nothing but atmosphere. If we could remove from the human organization flesh, blood and bones, we should still have membrane. Membrane music is perhaps the fitting expression of *Pelléas et Mélisande*.

> JAMES GIBBONS HUNEKER
> *New York Sun*, 1911

Neither Signor Verdi's music (which is Signor Verdi's worst) nor Mlle Piccolomini's singing (which everyone concedes is on a very small scale) have made the fame and furore of the opera and the lady. The music of *La Traviata* is trashy; and the young Italian lady cannot do justice to the music, such as it is. Hence it follows that the opera and the lady can only establish themselves in proportion as Londoners rejoice in a prurient story prettily acted.

> H.F. CHORLEY
> *The Athenaeum*, May 1856

It is the humanity in opera, however luridly implausible, that does the trick. Crude though so many libretti are and even more idiotic the plots, the man who invented opera had realised ... that the marriage of music and human beings lifts both into another realm altogether. Opera is *not* just wonderful sounds made flesh by words ... Take *The Magic Flute* alone. The plot is a mess and much of the dialogue is feeble and some unintelligible, yet we are transported to heaven not just because of the music, but because the music and words have fused into something greater than both, something indefinable but real.

> BERNARD LEVIN
> *The Times*, 14 November 1991

Verdi conduting one of his own operas

I attended an admirable concert recently and enjoyed myself very much, but whenever the singer was about to tackle a song in a foreign language I would cast my eyes at the translation of the words which was included in my program, and would see something like this: 'Beautiful lips, shuffling to and fro with indecision why don't you render me the delicious happiness to say yes, again yes, oh yes, lips, hurry up lips, yes, yes.' I am no great hand at understanding German and Italian, but I venture to say that the words of the songs were on a slightly higher literary level than the translations indicated.

Do you suppose that in Italy and Germany songs in English are translated in the same way for concert audiences? If so, I can imagine *Drink To Me Only With Thine Eyes* working out something like this: 'Let us agree, when drinking, to employ the eyeballs only; similarly with kisses; I sent you some flowers recently and you sent them back after breathing on them; they are still alive but are impregnated with your personal odour.'

Could UNESCO do anything about this confusing question of translating songs?

ROBERTSON DAVIES
*The Papers of Samuel Marchbanks*

The music of *Parsifal* is simply execrable. Gurnemanz is an absolute bore and Parsifal an insipid donkey.

J.W. DAVISON
to an unknown correspondent, 16 January 1883

After the senuous amours to the point of a *delirium tremens* of *Tristan*, gorged with aphrodisiac drugs, comes the *Valkyrie*, which offers us a repugnant spectacle of incestuous love, complicated by the adultery of a twin brother and sister.

O. COMETTANT
*Siècle*, March 1866

The almost impossible Tannhauser overture of Herr Richard Wagner introduced for the first time to an English audience and played with surprising accuracy and decision, would do very well for a pantomime or Easter piece. It is a weak parody of the worst compositions, not of M. Berlioz, but of his imitators. So much fuss about nothing, such pompous and empty commonplaces, has seldom been heard.

> J.W. DAVISON
> *The Times*, 3 May, 1854

Richard Wagner comes to London, an object of deeper curiosity ... than was any foreign musician who ever visited us; and, having had full scope, both as conductor and composer and opera director, for the vindication of his pretensions, he leaves ... convicted of making one of the profoundest failures on record.

> *Musical World*, June 1855

Alas for the music of Mahler! What a fuss about nothing! What a to-do about a few commonplace musical thoughts, hardly worthy of being called ideas.

> L.A. SLOPER
> *Christian Science Monitor*, Boston, January 1924

It is the work of a Communist travelling salesman.

> P-B GHÉUS, on Milhaud's opera *Maximilian*
> *Le Figaro*, January 1932

Reger might be epitomized as a composer whose name is the same either forward or backward, and whose music curiously displays the same characteristics.

> IRVING KOLODIN
> *New York Sun*, 1934

The Copland Piano Concerto is a harrowing horror from beginning to end. There is nothing in it that resembles music except as it contains noise – just as the words employed by Gertrude Stein may be said to resemble poetry because poetry consists of words, and so does her crazy clatter.
> *Boston Evening Transcript*, February 1927

The way to write American music is simple. All you have to do is to be an American and then write any kind of music you wish.
> VIRGIL THOMSON
> quoted in Machlis, *Introduction to American Music*

Mussorgsky was an amateur with moments of genius.
> SIR ERNEST NEWMAN
> quoted in *The Nation*, 1914

Rimsky-Korsakov – what a name! It suggests fierce whiskers stained with vodka.
> *Musical Courier*, New York 1897

He who would write the *Rite of Spring*
If I be right, by right should swing!
> *Boston Herald*, 1924

The orchestration of *Till Eulenspiegel* is sound and fury, signifying nothing.
> *Recorder*, New York 1896

It is not every family which has double fugues for breakfast, but this Strauss family is a peculiar one.
> LOUIS ELSON, on the *Sinfonia Domestica*
> *Boston Daily Advertiser*, 1917

It has been said that it is difficult to score a noise well. In his *Five Orchestral Pieces*, Schoenberg has certainly succeeded. There were passages that suggested a bomb in a poultry-yard, cackles, shrieks, caterwauls, and then – crash.

> LOUIS ELSON
> *Boston Daily Advertiser*, 1914

Gershwin's *An American in Paris* is nauseous claptrap, so dull, so patchy, thin, vulgar, long-winded and inane, that the average movie audience would be bored by it ... This cheap and silly affair seemed pitifully futile and inept.

> HERBERT F. PEYSER
> *New York Telegraph*, December 1920

I used to think that nightingales sang in tune until I discovered Stravinsky.

> graffiti in the Royal Academy of Music

After hearing Varése's *Ionization*, I am anxious that you should examine my composition scored for two stoves and a kitchen sink. I've named it *Concussion Symphony*, descriptive of the disintegration of an Irish potato under the influence of a powerful atomizer.

> Postcard signed Iona Lotta Bunk to Nicolas
> Slonimsky, July 1933, quoted in his *Lexicon of
> Musical Invective*.

On Saturday February 10th there was a singular novelty – nothing less than an attempt to illustrate the career of Napoleon on the pianoforte.

> *Monthly Musical Record*, March 1900

Two ladies, newly out of a West End London theatre, were discussing the 'musical' they had just seen. 'It's a funny thing,' one said to the other, 'but you can go into the theatre humming the hit numbers of Andrew Lloyd Webber's latest show before you've actually heard it.'
> ANON
> *Overheard on a London bus*, 1986


There flows through this form of entertainment a stream of mindlessness.
> JAMES AGATE, on musical comedy
> *Sunday Times*, August 1926


Some of the songs making the rounds now will be popular when Bach, Beethoven and Wagner are forgotten – but not before.
> LOUIS SOBEL
> New York newspaper columnist, *c.* 1950


The good composer is slowly discovered. The bad composer is slowly found out.
> SIR ERNEST NEWMAN


I fear I cannot say a good word of German music.
> SIR ARTHUR BLISS
> *What Modern Composition is Aiming At*


One day I'll be able to relax a bit, and try to become a good composer.
> BENJAMIN BRITTEN
> *Letter to Imogen Holst*, 1968

I respond very positively to certain birds. Especially eagles; and now I know from my experience in dreams that at some time in my past life I have been a bird of that particular kind, because I know exactly the feeling of flying and living in the body of that bird.

KARL-HEINZ STOCKHAUSEN
*Sunday Times*, 1973

Stravinsky rehearsing

Most composers bore me because most composers are boring.
>   SAMUEL BARBER

Not sung by Caruso, Jenny Lind, John MacCormack, Harry Lauder or the Village Nightingale.
>   CHARLES IVES
>   *Inscription on a Song*

Listening to Lloyd Webber's music will leave her (the Queen's) mind free to contemplate the next day's schedule. She will offer a silent prayer to God that she is not obliged to extend her very considerable intellect to concentrating too hard on something absolutely fatuous ... Lloyd Webber's music is extremely poor melodically and harmonically is extremely crude. He fails to touch emotion, and he has used every meretricious trick from Jesus Christ downward to make a fast buck.
>   MALCOLM WILLIAMSON
>   in a BBC 2 broadcast, quoted in *The Times*, 29
>   January 1992

Mr Andrew Lloyd Webber seems to be everywhere, but then so, I suppose, is Aids.
>   MALCOLM WILLIAMSON, Master of the Queen's Music
>   quoted in the *Glasgow Herald*, January 1992

They cut up timber, turning the lofty oak into sawdust.
>   ROBERT SCHUMANN on critics
>   *On Music and Musicians*

*Napoleon*: My dear Cherubini, you are certainly an excellent musician: but really, your music is so noisy and complicated, that I can make nothing of it.

*Cherubini*: My dear general, you are certainly an excellent soldier: but in regard to music, you must excuse me if I don't think it necessary to adapt my compositions to your comprehension.
> BELLAIS
> *Memorials of Cherubini*, 1874

Many people here think *Melusine* is my best overture; anyhow, it's the most intimate, but the rigmarole of the *Musikalische Zeitung* about red coral and magic castles and deep seas is all rubbish and astonishes me. All the same, I'm going to take leave of water for some time, and look around for other prospects.
> FELIX MENDELSSOHN
> in a letter to his sister, 30 January 1836

It is interesting to know the ideas, even the erroneous ideas, of geniuses, and men of great talent, such as Goethe, Schumann, Wagner, Saint-Beuve, and Michelet when they wish to indulge in criticism; but it is of no interest at all to know whether Mr So-and-so like, or does not like, such-and-such a dramatic or musical work.
> VINCENT D'INDY
> *Revue d'art dramatique*, February 1899

The Chorleys we have always with us: like Herodotus, I know their names but forbear to mention them. Chorley was an honourable man. So are they all honourable men. Peace be to their waste-paper baskets.
> SIR DONALD FRANCIS TOVEY
> *Essays in Musical Analysis*

Pay no attention to what the critics say. No statue has ever been put up to a critic.
> JEAN SIBELIUS

Critics love mediocrity.
    attributed to GIACOMO PUCCINI

All these lily-pad Doctors of Music!
    CHARLES IVES

I had ... a dream the other day about music critics. They were small and pack-like, with padlocked ears, as if they had stepped out of a painting by Goya.
    IGOR STRAVINSKY
    *Evening Standard*, 29 October 1969

If there is to be a chair for critics, I think it had better be an electric chair.
    SIR THOMAS BEECHAM